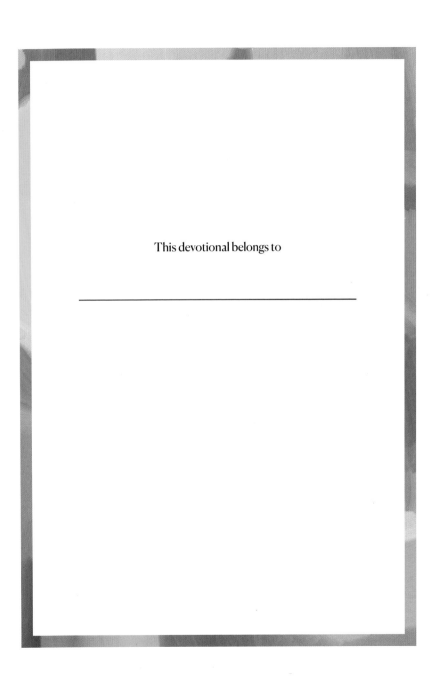

This devotional belongs to

_____

40 DAYS OF WALKING IN THE GOODNESS OF GOD

Abundant grace

TEXT BY WILL KASSNER
ART BY COURTNEY KASSNER

Founders of CREW + CO

Ink &
Willow

Contents

PART 1 | Knowing God's Grace

PART 2 | Trusting God's Grace

PART 3 | Showing God's Grace

Introduction

Life has a funny way of always taking us by surprise. Seasons come and go and are filled with steady change. In a world of chaos, finding a constant can be one of our greatest obstacles. So what keeps us grounded when we are surrounded by so much uncertainty?

When we first started our business, Crew + Co, life was filled to the brim with unknowns. We didn't know the future, but we were sure of one thing: We wanted our work to be a reflection of God's goodness. Through the highs and lows, ups and downs, our journey as business owners has been an in-color picture of the chaos of life. More than that, though, it has been a reflection of God's faithfulness.

All too often, we find ourselves overwhelmed or bogged down, drenched in the proverbial sweat of simply trying to get by. We get busy. We get tired. But all the while, God offers Himself to us, pouring out His goodness in the quiet moments of the morning and the busy moments of the afternoon. He is always near; we just have to take the time to see Him.

No one said life would be easy, but Jesus did remind us that He would not abandon us in it. He is our constant, our hope, and our joy. Though plenty of distractions will arise, we can always come back to the truth that He has overcome the world. When security seems to crumble like the last saltine cracker, we can always come back to His grace.

Abundant Grace is a forty-day journey of walking in the practical grace of God. Written with the daily grind in mind, these devotionals are designed to remind you of the one true constant: the hope we have in Christ. Each devotion ends with a space for reflection. Some close with questions to ponder, others with a prayer, and others with a prompt to dig into God's Word. Whatever the activity, may each one bring you greater awareness of and dependence on God's grace.

The hope of this book is to establish a routine and remembrance as you start each day. Even when we experience moments of feeling empty, we can set aside time throughout our day for moments to be filled because Jesus offers His grace in so many wonderful ways. We hope as you dive into this devotional and into His Word that you will see a new side of God's grace, waiting at the ready to fill your heart and refresh your soul.

Let's commit to slowing things down. To being intentional. To walking with Jesus over the next forty days, and to seeing how He leads us into His abundant grace.

PART 1

Knowing God's Grace

Grace abounded
all the more.

Romans 5:20

1 | Where Grace Begins

The best way to begin a journey is by taking inventory of the past. To truly move forward, you must first understand the path that has led you to where you are now. Perhaps, then, the best way to step into the magnitude of God's grace is to look back on the story of redemption, to recollect God's work from the beginning, and to remember that His goodness is nothing new. He is and has always been a God of grace.

From the beginning, God created us to know Him, but human hearts steadily drifted a different way. We can look back to the quiet morning in the Garden, which quickly erupted into chaos, as sin ran rampant from the choice of two to the hearts of many. Like an invasive vine, sin grew, choking out the peace that God so beautifully ushered into creation. As the world grew older, sin grew with it, slowly creeping to overcome the good that God had revealed in His work.

But the goodness of God could not be outdone, and God had a plan for a people He knew would fail—time and time again. Through years of waiting, of making promises and plans, God made this truth clear: though sin increases, grace increases all the more, poured out from a cup with endless supply. While the story of the Garden leads to exile and fear, the story of Jesus leads to glorious hope. For He came not to cast out, but to offer a way back home.

The journey of life is filled with hurdles, many of which lead us to question our purpose and God's plan. But we can look back to remember the story and the promise, because those reminders are often what carry us in moments of frustration or defeat.

When Jesus feels distant, remember that we are the ones who walk away. (Trust me, we've *all* been there.) When He feels inconsistent, remember His grace has always been steady. Our lives are wrapped up in the fullness and glory of what Jesus has revealed—a salvation we could never earn on our own. We can rejoice in the truth that His grace was, and is, always greater.

Reflect | *How have you overlooked the importance of God's grace in your own life? What are ways that you have minimized your need for His renewal and redemption?*

Those who dwell at the ends of the earth are in awe at your signs.

Psalm 65:8

River of Grace

If you have never tried fly fishing, this is me telling you it's time to give it a go (seriously, let me know and I'll come with). The beauty of fly fishing is that catching fish is not even the best part. There is a magic in being surrounded by the river's rumble, by the poetry in motion as water rushes over glassy rocks and sandy banks. The soothing juxtaposition of water washing over unkept ground offers a beautiful picture of renewal moving along unhindered at your feet. Because there's just something about a river that calms the troubled mind.

We've all had days when we feel like we've used up every drop of redemptive water and that nothing is left to refresh or refine our own lives. We've all met that person in the mirror and thought, *I'm not sure what God could do to fix this!* Our hearts often fill with questions like *How could God have anything left to give?* or *Surely, I ran out of second chances the last time?*

But on those days, remember that we are the ones standing with our backs turned to the water, our fingers in our ears, somehow convinced there is not enough grace in God's river to fully restore and renew us. But contrary to our doubts, the river of God's grace is swiftly flowing and always abounding, washing over the troubles of yesterday, quenching the thirst of pain, and strengthening our hearts for tomorrow. We simply have to step into the water and let Him do the work. His grace washes over our shortcomings and failures, renewing our souls into well-polished stones.

So instead of wondering what God has left to give, let's roll up our pant legs and wade on in. God is with us—of that we have no reason to doubt. May the rushing waters of His grace revive your soul.

Meditate | *Read Psalm 65. Which of God's characteristics stand out to you? How do you see Him at work in the world around you?*

For I desire steadfast love and not sacrifice, the knowledge of God rather than burnt offerings.

Hosea 6:6

Don't Check the Box

Checking the box can be a slippery slope. As kids, we clean our rooms with grumbling words, hastily throwing clothes under the bed to get the job done. As adults, well, we do the same thing. Whether cleaning a room, working that nine-to-five, or studying for the next test, we are often satisfied with the minimum requirement.

The trouble is, when we approach God in this manner, we overlook the depth of what He is truly offering. We may read the Bible or a devotional and think, *All good, God, I'm ready for you to bless me now!* but the reality of knowing God runs much deeper than a to-do list. God is asking far more of us than simply going through the motions.

Throughout the Old Testament narrative, we see several instances when box-checking is confused with obedience (1 Samuel 11, Hosea 6). This age-old mistake of going through the motions stems from the common misconception that forgiveness comes from simply following the rules. Old Testament redemption was largely tied to sacrifice, but often, people missed the reality behind the ritual. The sacrifice in and of itself was not the source of redemption; it was merely a picture of what God was doing tangibly in their hearts.

You see, trusting in God and accepting forgiveness do not begin with outward actions. On the contrary, true peace with God begins in the heart. When we surrender our hearts to Him, we begin to find what we could never work to achieve. The simplest of solutions to one of life's greatest predicaments is this: To find true renewal, we must first surrender. Redemption does not come by following a list or reluctantly doing what God thinks is best (He sees your eye rolls!). It comes from giving up control and recognizing our dependence on Him.

God longs for us to obey Him because we love Him, not because of a self-righteous or proud desire to "check a box." We can strive to appear like we have it together, but we gain so much more when we submit to His will and allow Him to lead.

Obedience over sacrifice, love over ritual. These are the daily hallmarks of surrendering to God. So don't settle for the surface; don't just check the box.

Reflect | *Where have you been guilty of box checking? When has ego or reputation been more important than obedience in your life? How can you be more honest with God in your pursuit of Him?*

And the Word became flesh.

John 1:14

God Doesn't Need Our Spectacular

Our church had three double-wide trailers in the back parking lot for the youth and college ministries, a location which earned the affectionate nickname "The Outback." Filled with secondhand couches and dented metal chairs, those trailers were far from fancy. But the space became a sanctuary, a refuge from the noise of life and a reflection of our own personal imperfections. We prayed and sang and poured our hearts out, unhindered by the distraction of our humble surroundings. We were simply there to meet with God.

We may give them undivided attention, but exteriors are vastly overrated. I mean, what in life really matters, anyway? Our deepest experiences of joy come from moments when we disregard the trivial and focus on the personal. Conversations are deeper when we forget the dishes in the sink or the dust on the light fixtures (just kidding—we aren't looking up there!) and instead focus on the person across the table. After all, the imperfect is often the place where we most feel known and understood.

We often think of God as unapproachable, but the paradox of glorious presence in a humble venue has always been in His repertoire. Ironically, He is known for stepping in where we least expect. From the throne of heaven to the filth of hay, He took on flesh that we might know Him. From a crown of glory to a sorrowful heart, He took on pain so that He might suffer with us. We do not serve a God who needs our spectacular, our fancy, or our bedazzled. We see and know and love a Savior who meets us exactly where we are, no questions asked.

Jesus is not a distant deity who withdrew from our mishaps, but a personal Savior who meets us where we are, dirty couches and all.

Meditate | *Read John 1. How does Jesus's human experience encourage you to approach Him honestly?*

He is before
all things
and in him
all things
hold together.

Colossians 1:17

It's All in His Hands

Uncontrolled variables are the kryptonite to the modern-day world. As long as everything works, we're sure to have a great day. But what happens when the tire goes flat or the pizza is late? What happens when you order pretzels from the grocery store and they drop off chocolate chips?

As much as we want to be in control, we are constantly bombarded by reminders that we are not. Our response to those reminders should not be to pine for more stability, but to live in a greater attitude of surrender. Our outlook should be a big-picture, panoramic, space-satellite view—one that reveals the world does not revolve around us, but Him.

This world was made through Jesus; and thankfully, through Jesus, it is being reconciled back to Him. He is the glory of God revealed, the perfect picture of grace, the promise of life. And in Him all things hold together. We have nothing to fear because of the work He has done, and we have nothing to fear because of the work He is still doing. In Jesus, we have all our strength, hope, and joy. He was not *just* a man who walked this earth, not *just* a teacher filled with knowledge. He was God in the flesh, who, in humility, took on human form and submitted to death on the cross. He is our Resurrected King, who conquered death and brings redemption to all who believe.

By Him this world was created, and by Him this world will be made new. When your days get caught up in the struggle of stress, or when your heart feels heavy with the burdens of your friends, take a moment to remember who Jesus is. He has not left us or abandoned us, but has made Himself knowable. He holds us up, breathes life into our lungs, and sets joy in our hearts. He knows our hurts and hears our prayers.

Whenever you feel like life is out of control, remember that it is all in His hands.

Pray

Jesus, You are before all things, in all things, and with us in all things. Remind me of who You are and fill me with the joy and peace only You can give. Help me to remember the hope we have in You.

See what kind of love the Father has given to us.

1 John 3:1

Day

6 | He Loves Us Anyway

As parents, the most common question we hear in our house is, "When can I have dessert?" Without a doubt, our kids ask this every single day. Our response, more often than not, is based on the kids' actions and choices that precede the daily inquiry. (Conditional reward at its finest, right?)

But have you ever stopped to think what life would be like if God's love was conditional? How far would God be from us if His grace depended on what we did? We need His love, but if we are honest, not one of us deserves it. We long for grace and hope, but by our own power, we have no means of obtaining either.

Thankfully, God's love is not based on conditions. It is not based on circumstances or choices we make, but on who He is. He loves us because that is His nature. He loves us because we are His workmanship, created to know the depths of His unending grace. The whole of humanity's purpose can be summed up in one powerful point: to see and know and experience God.

When we ask God for more of Him, He does not hold back. He does not reply with a self-help program or a New Year's resolution. When we ask, He gives and gives. When we pray, He listens. When we are broken, He mends. When we are hopelessly hurting, He offers us hope. Merely because we measure others by their actions does not mean God does the same. His love is unearned yet unyielding, constantly chipping away at the pride of our callous hearts.

It is in our nature to be imperfect, but it is not in His. And in His perfect love, we rejoice because our joy is not set on conditions, but in a Savior who gave Himself up for our sake. He is the God of promise, of mercy and grace. Despite all our shortcomings, He loves us anyway.

Reflect | *In what areas are you holding on to guilt when you should be letting go? How are you moving guilt aside to make room for joy? How can you forgive yourself as God has forgiven you?*

For all his works
are right
and his ways
are just.

Daniel 4:37

His Kingdom, Not Our Own

In the good and the bad, God is still working. His redemptive story doesn't stop when things get ugly. Even through hardships and difficulties, He promises to make all things new. Even though many times we can't see how, His works are right and His ways are trustworthy.

For me, seasons of waiting have always been hard. In those times, I feel like God isn't listening, so out of frustration I begin to forge my own way. After all, if God won't do something, then I guess I'll get things moving myself! But when I get frustrated with God or overly focused on myself, I can end up in a pretty uncomfortable place.

In Daniel's account of King Nebuchadnezzar, we see a man at the end of his rope. He wanted his kingdom to thrive, and he was going to stop at nothing to see it done—until God stepped in. The wild events in Nebuchadnezzar's life (he moved in with cows, for crying out loud!) led him to the realization that God was in control. Life found him in a hard place, but God used that hard place to make His goodness known.

As with Nebuchadnezzar's life, our stories are more than what happens to us today. God often uses our circumstances to reveal more of His grace and remind us of our dependency on Him. For us, it is vitally important to remember our hope is not in a God who separated Himself from us, but in One who suffered for our sake. In His righteousness, He met us at our worst so that we might experience His best.

He may not have you grazing in a pasture like a cow, but you may be in a tough season nonetheless. So in your waiting, wandering, or wanting, remember He is God and you are not. Don't let the desire to build your own kingdom outweigh your heart for His grace.

His ways are good—in that we can trust. His ways are right—in that we can hope.

Meditate | *Read Daniel 4:28–37. How have you been seeking to build your kingdom over God's? How can you surrender your goals and ambitions to Him?*

For my thoughts are not your thoughts, neither are your ways my ways, declares the Lord.

Isaiah 55:8

Let God Be God

God is beyond us. His understanding is bigger than ours. He is wonderful to behold.

Why, then, do we try to break God down to work on our level? Why do we insist that God do things our way? Sure, we want immediate results. Of course, we crave instant satisfaction. Our culture has conditioned us to see delay as a sign of failure. My phone needs an upgrade, and my shoes are so last year—and don't tell me two-day shipping isn't an option! Seize the day and get more stuff!

With the world at our fingertips, we are often left wondering why God can't be there, too. My apps hear voice commands instantly, so why does it sometimes feel as though God isn't hearing my prayers? If we aren't careful, we can find ourselves letting our understanding of God be limited to the "give me more blessings" mentality—and, as a result, we might miss the truth that *He* is the blessing. He is what our hearts are after.

Our joy does not come from playing God, from putting ourselves on His level, or from pretending like we know better than He does. In fact, the more we live to satisfy our own cravings, the emptier we become. Our joy does not come from self-fulfillment. It comes from resting in His sovereignty, in His constant control, and in His perfect peace.

He is more than we deserve, yet He is all we will ever need. He is more than we can ever know, yet He makes Himself knowable. He is beyond what has been revealed, yet in His grace, He has revealed His goodness. His character contains so much mystery, but we can still experience His majesty. He is beyond us, yet every day He keeps close beside us. He is our blessing, and He is good.

Pray

God, help me see Your goodness and Your joy in each day. Give me patience in waiting and satisfaction in Your presence. I don't want to be captivated by consuming. I want to be overwhelmed by Your love.

The Lord, the Lord, a God merciful and gracious, slow to anger, and abounding in steadfast love and faithfulness.

Exodus 34:6

9 | God Does Not Hide His Glory

How would you describe God? Could you put into words the ways He has worked in your life? Or maybe He seems too distant and aloof to describe at all. Here is the crux: the vastness of God's glory does not depend on our experience. He simply is exactly who He is. Yet His glory is available to all who ask.

In Exodus 33, Moses begs God not for security or safety but for the comfort of His presence. Israel had turned their backs on God, and in a desperate plea for forgiveness, Moses simply and humbly asked God to stay with them. He could have said, "God, don't leave—my reputation is on the line," or "If you leave, I might look like a failure." But rather than consider how he might look to others, he focused on his deepest need: more of God's presence. Even in desperation, at risk of abandonment and failure, he knew his greatest reward was to know more of God.

In response, God did just as Moses asked. He passed by in a radiant light and spoke the words describing Himself: full of mercy and steadfast love, faithful and gracious. The experience brought Moses so near to God that, as he descended the mountain, his face shone with the glory of God. Moses asked, and God revealed exactly who He was: near and present, true and just, mighty and powerful over all things.

We often base our understanding of God on who we think He should be, instead of allowing Him to reveal Himself to us. Instead of asking Him, we form our own opinions. The danger of forming those opinions accrues as we base our understanding of God on our own character instead of His.

Fortunately, we don't have to look hard to find out exactly who God is. He is constantly revealing Himself to us—through creation, His Word, and His Spirit. He will not hold back from those who seek His face. May our prayer be to see more of His glory.

Reflect | *What are the first attributes that come to mind when you think of God? What thoughts do you have about God that are based more on your own circumstances and less on His character?*

You will seek me
and find me,
when you seek me
with all your heart.

Jeremiah 29:13

Day

10 | Give God Your Best

New skills are, for me, often daunting (just check my honey-do list). I get nervous about learning something new, and inevitably doubt creeps in. From there, the thought, *What if I'm not good enough?* often hinders success. Sometimes I'll delay a project just because it feels uncomfortable or out of my league (and by delay, I'm talking years!).

The good news of God's grace is that it doesn't have to be within our ability to earn or achieve. Restoration comes through His faithfulness as the fulfillment of His promise. The joy that comes from such rich restoration is best experienced when our lives reflect His good and when we set our hearts in obedience to Him.

In Jeremiah's letter to the exiles, we see the beauty of God's promise. Even while living under foreign rule in a foreign land, God promised Israel a future of hope and renewal. God was not done yet, and He would reveal His grace even in the middle of divine discipline. Although God sent Israel to a foreign land, He did not give them over to foreign rules. He did not expect perfection, but He did ask for their hearts. The beautiful reminder for the exiles was that God was going with them, and the more they committed themselves to Him, the more of Him they would find.

In many ways, we share a similar situation (spiritually speaking) as exiles in a foreign land. Often, we feel held back by what we can achieve on our own. With so much wrong in the world, how could we ever hope to make a difference? And if our efforts can't make an impact, what is even the point? But more than your actions, more than the good you can create, God is after your heart. Our first step is to surrender, and from there we can join gladly in His work—no fear or doubt attached.

So give Him your best, confident that He is greater than any of your flaws, and that He is faithful despite any of your failures.

Reflect | *What is something you are holding on to that you need to surrender to God? What is holding you back from giving Him your best?*

Fear not, for I have redeemed you; I have called you by name, you are mine.

Isaiah 43:1

11 | Grace Is Not Earned

I threw up during a football game in eighth grade. (That moment lives rent-free in my mind, one of those core memories I wish I could forget but which has somehow staked its claim in the bedrock of my memory.) After the game, my coach gave me the highly coveted "player of the week" shirt. These shirts were typically reserved for the running backs, the playmakers, or the all-stars—but on that night, I got my shirt. It felt undeserved, unearned, and unmerited. I had not done anything but get sick. But I'll never forget when my coach looked at me and said, "Great job—you (literally) left it all on the field."

God's grace is a lot like that moment. We can never earn salvation. If anything, the best we can do is simply give up trying. Why try so hard to achieve or succeed when God simply asks us to surrender? After all, when we try to reach perfection, we only find ourselves further and further from it. The beauty of grace comes in the truth that our imperfections are met with His unending faithfulness, and that our constant failure is overcome with His constant forgiveness. Jesus doesn't just offer to make us better versions of ourselves; He offers to transform us from the inside out. A true process of sanctification, a redeeming work that shapes and molds us to be more like Him.

We cannot take credit for what God has done in our lives, but by His kindness, He allows us to walk in the benefits. He is constantly at work in our hearts, drawing us to Himself and revealing His love to us. He knows us by name, and He has made us His own. He invites us to leave behind our pride and self-righteous esteem—and He gives us His grace like a super cool "player of the week" t-shirt. Where grace could not be earned, it is freely given.

Reflect | *In what areas of your life are you trying too hard? How can you focus more on grace and less on work?*

I wait for the Lord, my soul waits, and in his word I hope.

Psalm 130:5

Day

12 | Wait with Grace

One thing is true in life, a commonality we can all count on. At some point, we are going to have to wait. We have all been there, and most likely we will be there again. Maybe we're waiting for something big, like the next job, the next house, or the next dream. Maybe our wait is for something small, like our coffee order or the release of that next great song. No matter the importance, waiting plays a fundamental constant in every single day. We have no choice but to wait. But we *can* choose whether we wait in patience or pessimism.

We can wait expectantly, knowing that God's ways are not our ways, assured by His grace that He will lead the way. We can wait gladly, confident that He is fulfilling His promise to redeem. We can also wait in anger, frustrated with God's lack of answer to our many desperate prayers. We can wait in frustration, wondering what exactly God is doing in our lives, and feeling discouraged at our lack of control.

Is it justified to be frustrated in certain seasons? Of course. Is it natural to grow impatient? Certainly. We all have moments of weakness, but we shouldn't let the discouragement of waiting steal the reality of our joy. In His grace, God has revealed enough that we can know He is near even when we feel as though we have been forgotten. He has given us His Word, living and active, by which we can fill our hearts with what is true and beautiful and good. He has revealed Himself and has shown His grace, so that when we feel the loneliest and most forgotten, we can still cling to Him. Against all odds we can wait in hope, even when all hope seems lost. We can rest in difficulty because God is exactly who He said He is.

So don't let frustration rule your heart. Hope in His Word and rest in His truth. He is worth the wait.

Meditate | *Read Psalm 130. Meditate on the refreshing grace that flows from God's Word. Breathe deep and rest in Him.*

PART 2

Trusting God's Grace

Cast your burden on the Lord, and he will sustain you.

Psalm 55:22

God Is Not a Last Resort

How often do you try everything you can in your own power before asking God for help? Do you ever think, *I've got this, God. When it gets really bad, I'll call you.*

Despite how we might treat Him, God is not merely a lifeline to grab when we've reached the limit of self-sufficiency. He is not our best shot at an escape plan. Quite the opposite, actually. He is the very vessel that holds us up in the middle of the storm. By the graciousness of His colossal love, He does not leave us to wander this world alone or in aimless misery. He designed us, with full intention and individuality, to know Him fully as He fully knows us.

We often approach God as desert wanderers: empty, tired, thirsty, and dry (sort of like you might feel after leaving the house without your water bottle). We wait until we have nothing left and condition ourselves to call on Him only when there is a circumstantial need. But when we write God off as our emergency red phone, we miss much of what He has intended for us to experience.

The aim of life should not be for God to make things easy. The aim, and the adventure, is to know Him more. The fullness of life comes when we realize that God is relational and that we become our best selves when we *lose* ourselves. Life becomes most enjoyable when we focus on ourselves less. God is available and attentive to our needs. He is a friend, ready to lift the weight of our burdensome load.

Reach out to Him for the joy of knowing Him. Remember, He is not a last resort.

Pray | *God, help me to seek You first and lay my burdens before You. Help me to rest in Your ability, and not in my own.*

For where your treasure is, there will your heart be also.

Luke 12:34

14 | Put Jesus on Your Schedule

We live in a culture that demands we move fast or get left behind. The motto of today is centered on what I can get ready for tomorrow. And so we're constantly scrambling—on the grind for the next big thing.

In a culture that is centered on speed, when was the last time you slowed things down? When was the last time you intentionally set aside time to seek Jesus? Of course, we all have a to-do list two miles long (There are bills to pay, for crying out loud!). Our daily tasks often weigh heavier on our hearts than they should. We live in the temporary and forget we were designed for the eternal. We forget that Jesus is our greatest reward.

Though our days often feel like they have a shortage of hours, we shouldn't be afraid to be intentional with our time. We shouldn't run ourselves ragged in responsibility, all the while missing the reality that God wants to engage with us. We shouldn't settle for empty when our souls could simmer full, bubbling over with the grace He supplies. God offers us the joy of His presence, but we must be willing to give Him the time.

But how do we do this on a practical level when the world demands so much of our attention? Well, we can take our Bibles to work and read on our lunch break. We can recite verses at the red light that always takes too long to change. We can pray over our coworkers instead of talking bad about them. We can go for a walk and listen to God whisper in the wind. We can fight the urge to rush through the day and instead slow down and sit with Him. We can be reminded that Jesus is our treasure and delight.

Instead of fretting over the next big thing, soak in the sweet simplicity of His grace. Give Him your day, and you'll be surprised at the fullness you find.

What has been filling your calendar recently? How does Jesus factor into your daily schedule? How could you intentionally restructure your day to spend more time with Him?

For everything
there is a season,
and a time for
every matter
under heaven.

Ecclesiastes 3:1

15 | He Is with Us

When has God been nearest to you? Do you tend to experience God's presence more during "high" seasons or "low" ones? Are you drawn more deeply into daily communion with Him when life is going great or when it's falling to pieces around you? Does God ever feel distant when everything seems to be shifting too quickly for you to handle?

If you're like me, remembering to watch and wait for God during seasons of change can be challenging. Trusting in God can feel easy when life is good, but it can be hard when nothing goes according to plan. In the moment, we may find it difficult to discern God's grace. We may struggle to see through our tears of pain. We might have to fight to focus when the chaos of life only seems to build. But remember this: God is in everything, and He is with us in everything. He is present and caring, directing and guiding us as we go and grow. Thankfully, our feelings do not impact the nearness of His grace.

Change definitely makes life hard, but it also makes life beautiful. There may be seasons when we feel like God is tearing us down, but we're sure to experience seasons when He will build us back up. He is the master builder, the artist at work, growing us in the grace He calls us to reflect. He walks with us, holds us up, and encourages us to step forward in faith day by day.

You may be in a season of great joy, or you may be in a season of immense hurt. Wherever you find yourself today, remember not to set your hope on current— or even future—circumstances. In our weakness, our brokenness, and our desperation, He is consistently close. Though seasons change, the promise of His presence never does. No matter the circumstances, God is always with us.

Reflect | *How would you define your current season? Within that season, how have you been trusting in God's grace? How have you been content in letting Him lead?*

Look at the birds
of the air:
they neither sow
nor reap nor gather
into barns, and yet
your heavenly Father
feeds them. Are you
not of more value
than they?

Matthew 6:26

Today Is Not Your Burden to Manage

Have you ever sat outside on a sunny winter day, adrift between the icy breeze and the pleasantly warm sun? For me, that's about as good as it gets. Just look at those birds up in those trees . . . oops, got distracted there for a minute. Let's get this thought train back on track.

When you woke up today, where did your thoughts go first? Maybe your mind went immediately to God's goodness and new mercies. Perhaps, if you're more like me, you floated through a sea of random wanderings (cue the birds). Or maybe your thoughts were quickly captivated by the running list of worries, responsibilities, and tasks that are already filling up today's plate. If any of these describes you, take heart. God knew exactly how our minds would work, which is why—in His grace—He gave us encouraging passages like Matthew 6.

In this chapter, which is part of the larger Sermon on the Mount, Jesus explains how birds depend on God's provision instead of worrying their feathers off about where their next meal or shelter is going to come from. On and on they fly, exactly as they were intended to do.

With this example, Jesus draws a parallel to our own lives and how we should live them: not in worry, but with trust in Him and in His grace. Instead of filling our time with fret or feverish hurry, Jesus invites us to live in constant worship. From the time we wake up to the time we go to sleep, no matter the circumstances, we can abide in Him. We can get lost in the beauty of who He has made us to be. We are His own, and He has made us to know His goodness.

Wherever your mind drifts today, remember this: Today is not your burden to manage. Instead of choosing worry, choose instead to hum a song of praise, to reflect in thankfulness while sipping a cup of coffee, and to enjoy that sunshine for just a few minutes longer.

Meditate

Read Matthew 6:25–34. How does this passage resonate with you? How is worry or control holding you back from experiencing God's grace?

So we do not lose heart. Though our outer self is wasting away, our inner self is being renewed day by day.

2 Corinthians 4:16

Your Mundane Matters

Ordinary days can often feel monotonously repetitive in a way that makes us long for something more important or extravagant. We want the highlights, but we're left with the dull drag of every play in between. How many times can the laundry possibly need to be done? Is there really another dish to wash? Are the kids hungry again? Ordinary can be exhausting, but it can also be fulfilling. For even in the monotony, God's grace is waiting for us.

Our outlook on the ordinary says much about our perspective on God's goodness and provision. Those little moments each day may be repetitive, but they also provide opportunities for discipleship, service, and living out Christ-like love. For the grind is where we get to know Jesus. We may feel like time is wasting away, but these are the days when God refreshes and reforms, redeems and renews.

Jesus didn't need the spotlight to be patient and kind. He listened and genuinely cared. He sought out the unwanted, the forgotten, and the overlooked. He touched the sick, the poor, and the untouchable. He poured out His grace in the ordinary, as an example for how we should also live.

So the next time you wash the dishes, wash them with the reminder of God's constant forgiveness and cleansing mercy. Feed the kids with the reminder of God's nourishment and the filling sustenance that comes from His Word. Fold laundry with care and kindness, as God over and over shows kindness to us. Love people with the reminder of how Jesus did.

Our actions in the mundane are what define our responses to the big moments. The "ordinary" days are when we most deeply influence and lead, often unknowingly, those around us. Don't miss out on the blessings God can bring in the little moments.

Reflect

Where do you see joy in the ordinary today? What are things you do every day that could turn into an opportunity to reflect God's grace?

This is the day that the Lord has made; let us rejoice and be glad in it.

Psalm 118:24

Life Is a Gift

Stress rules the world, or at least it seems. We're all bound to it like a dog on a leash, constantly being pulled back by the bleakness of tomorrow. We're burdened by what we don't know. We're burdened by what we *do* know. The future is coming for us, and it's coming with an army of hardship and hurdles.

You may be in the thick of raising toddlers who don't sleep or teenagers who don't listen. You may be struggling to find recognition at work or drowning in responsibilities that continually seem to add up. You may be trying to figure out how to come to terms with the illness the doctor just read from his chart. I heard a friend jokingly say he watches his 401k shrink every day . . . except I'm not sure he was joking. Plenty of things bring us down. But just because stress exists doesn't mean we have to give it control.

So how do we deal with this stress? Simply put, we recognize life's simple joys. Think about it: There's a beautiful joy in the simplicity of life, the freedom of taking that next deep breath. Life is a gift, a present in the present, each and every moment of the day. In all the noise that surrounds us, a quiet freedom is whispered in our hearts: He is our joy.

To know God is to live to the fullest. To sit in His presence is a gift outweighing all others. But watching the sunrise, sharing stories with a friend, eating a home-cooked meal, or laughing for hours on end are all gifts from Him, too. We can call out in prayer on the hardest of days knowing that He is listening, knowing that He has overcome. We can sing praises in the deepest of pain, resting in the assurance of His grace.

We may not know what tomorrow will bring, but we can be certain that, if tomorrow comes, it will be a gift from Him.

Pray

God, I give You the burdens of my heart. Help me to trust that You will carry them. Fill me with the grace to persevere. Help me to enjoy my days as the gift they are. Remind me of Your steadfast love.

But godliness
with contentment
is great gain.

1 Timothy 6:6

Day

19 | Consistently Content

On rainy days, the roof of my car leaks. The leak isn't too bad (yet), just a steady drip to remind me that things in life aren't quite perfect.

We are surrounded by imperfections we would love to fix or improve. Ironically enough, all these imperfections have to be met with our limitations. More often than not, our things-to-improve list is a vastly bigger problem than our bank account's ability to solve. Cars break and medical bills come in. Air conditioners go out and the credit card balance comes in. The question for us is not about the level of our limitations (hey, you may have won the lottery last week), but how we respond in contentment to those limitations.

Contentment, after all, is a funny concept. We can want and buy and need and fix for the rest of our lives and never have quite enough. There is always a better version, a more pristine model, a higher-quality option. But our hearts were not designed to be overwhelmingly captivated by the material. Our hearts were made to be satisfied in sanctification and in the beautiful journey of walking closely with God.

The truth is, we have already been made rich in the grace of God. The difficulty is in sacrificing our material desires to recenter our dreams around kingdom living. Our greatest attribute is not the house we live in or the car we drive, but the love of Jesus that has been given to each one of us so that we can reflect it to others. If God has blessed you with much, be content to give much away. If God has given you little, remember that even on the hard days He is immeasurably pouring out His grace. We can enjoy life in seasons of plenty and in seasons of need. We can find peace in the love He has richly given. His grace is not bound by limitations, and when we live in contentment, we can gain so much of Him.

What nonessential thing or experience have you been wanting to buy recently? How might you spend the money to bless others instead?

Where were you when I laid the foundation of the earth?

Job 38:4

20 | He Has a Plan

In the span of a single year, I was turned down for two jobs I was certain God had saved just for me. I waited for six months from the interview to the bad-news phone call in both instances, strung out on the hope that this time things would work out. It was a soul-crushing time, one filled with far more questions than answers. It felt like every move I made was wrong, like the weight of the world was on my shoulders, and like I was trapped in a spin cycle of worry and doubt.

Looking back now, so much of my waiting makes sense, since God used it to lead me to a place of dependency and trust. When I finally settled down and put my full trust in God, He graciously showed me the way. I was doing my best to bulldoze a path for the future, but I eventually realized God had already laid the path I needed to take. In hindsight, I can confidently say He had my best in mind.

In the heat of the moment, perspective is a difficult lens to shift. We can get caught up in the "I can't" and forget to think about the "He can." Job fought this battle as he wrestled with God, asking over and over, "Why? How could life possibly come to this?" But at the sound of God's voice, Job was silent, understanding at last the reality in which we all live: God is always in control.

No one says life is easy. If we are honest, it is a wild ride of hardship and uncertainty. But mixed within all the hardship is the grace of God that meets us and fills us exactly where we are. We know and love and worship a God who holds us in His hands, who pours out abundant grace all the days of our lives. He knows us deeply; He understands our needs and our desires. Even when we may not sense it, He is at work in our lives. We can relax in His grace, for He always has a plan.

Pray

Jesus, help me see You at work on the difficult days. Help me feel the renewal of Your grace during difficult seasons and trust in You every day. When I cannot see what lies ahead, remind me of Your faithfulness.

Therefore, my beloved brothers, be steadfast, immovable, always abounding in the work of the Lord, knowing that in the Lord your labor is not in vain.

1 Corinthians 15:58

Day 21 | Your Work in the Lord Is Not in Vain

One day when I was in elementary school, my mom made homemade chocolate chip cookies. I thought they were for my siblings and me, but to my disappointment, she had baked them for one of her coworkers. But when she came home, my mom was discouraged and defeated. The woman had thrown the cookies in the trash. My mother's kindness had been rejected, and it hurt immensely (also, what a waste of delicious cookies!).

So often we do kind things based on the surefire results we hope to receive. We do nice things to get a nice response. But what about when our kindness is rejected? What happens when others pull away and we feel the sting of embarrassment?

Let's face it: Being kind can be difficult, especially when we don't receive kindness in return. When we encounter rudeness or dissension, responding in grace is hard. Responding in pride is always much easier. Pride permits us to lash out, to turn our backs, and to discard and dismiss. Though it may be in our nature to live on the defensive, our calling in grace is to press in—to give ourselves away, even when others reject our love.

The call to being kind and serving others is an uphill climb. It is the continual laying down of ourselves, a dying to self, and an understanding that our lives are best lived when we give them away. We won't always see the results, and the outcome is not always what we hope, but we can still trust that God is at work in the hearts of others. He can do more with a little faith than we could do with a lifetime of pride.

Remember that Jesus Himself experienced rejection and pain. He is not merely familiar with sacrifice; He is the standard for it. In His perfection, He gave all of Himself—even His life—that we might know the richness of His grace. Hold fast, even though you may be rejected, overlooked, or unseen. You may feel defeated, but God is not outdone. You may feel empty, but God is faithful to fill you up. Keep serving, for your work is not in vain.

 Reflect | *How can you serve someone this week who might be difficult to love? How can you find ways to serve those around you with no expectation of receiving anything in return?*

God is our
refuge and strength,
a very present help
in trouble.
Psalm 46:1

Day

22 | Fear Should Not Define Us

A healthy fear plays a pivotal role for most of us. A fear of heights keeps us safely behind the ledge. A fear of burning keeps us (most of the time) from putting our hands in a fire. In many ways, fear keeps us cautiously grounded and offers a rationale behind good decision-making and bad. I suppose you could call it a cognitive safety net.

But what happens when fear takes control, when we lose ourselves to the weight of the unknown and collapse into constant worry?

So much of life is out of our control. We can't control tomorrow, but sometimes fear convinces us to try anyway. I've been caught in a panic many times a day with the notion that everything depends on me—which leads to my stomach hurting, heart pounding, blood pressure rising—none of which changes the outcome of anyone's day (except maybe mine . . . in a negative way). Fear tricks us into thinking our inability will lead to failure. But we are not bound to fear, for we can rejoice in the truth that all our doubt is met with His grace.

When fear surrounds us, remember God is with us and is a refuge for those in trouble, a shelter for those who are tired, and a friend for those who are afraid. When our hearts are broken, when our strength has waned, He picks up the pieces and puts us back together. When we feel unheard, He is still listening.

So instead of focusing on fear, dig into the trustworthiness of His Word. Pray the truth of His long-standing faithfulness over your doubt. Sing His praises even when it feels like no solution is in sight. Set fear aside and focus on His promise of grace. Time and time again you will find your fears subside in the familiarity of His faithfulness.

Meditate

Read Psalm 46. What comforts you in these verses? How does God's faithfulness in Scripture encourage you to seek His faithfulness today?

Standing fast
in the Lord.

1 Thessalonians 3:8

Day 23 | Hold Steady, Press On

Running offers an incredible parallel to the spiritual life. If you're a runner, you understand the crazy mental game you play on just about every venture. No matter how long or short the run, at some point you are going to want to stop. The sun might be blazing down on you, your feet might start hurting, or your side might start cramping (literally the worst!). You might have plenty of reasons to quit, and you will definitely reach the point when stopping seems like a better alternative to pushing through.

Spiritually, the struggle is quite the same. Even on the best days, we might hit moments of weakness, brokenness, or sheer fatigue. We may have to fight the urge to live for ourselves instead of considering the needs of others. We may become torn between seeking His good and wanting our gain. We may encounter such heartbreaking disappointment that we want to throw in the towel and walk away.

But no great (or mediocre, for that matter) runner ever crossed the finish line with the luxury of ease. To keep going, a runner has to double down—*left foot, right foot, breathe in, breathe out.*

The difficulty with our spiritual race is that we often feel the pressure to accomplish something great to please God. Many of us get so transfixed by some spiritual peak or pinnacle that we feel bad or guilty when we can only focus on the next step. We correlate our fatigue with failure.

Hear this: We all get tired. We all have moments of doubt. But our relationship with God is a journey, a marathon. And just because you're tired does not mean you have to give up. There will be days when the goal seems ephemeral and distant, too far to ever reach. When all you can think is, *I'm tired, God,* remember to reach out for the hydrating grace only He can give—a grace that will quench your thirst and satisfy your soul.

On days of weakness, don't be overwhelmed by the task that lies ahead. Take your race one step at a time and keep moving forward in the grace He gives. Let's push through today in the hope we have in Jesus.

Left foot, right foot—His grace is enough.

What obstacle is weighing you down or filling you with exhaustion right now? How can you cultivate time with God to guard your heart against spiritual fatigue?

Continue steadfastly
in prayer,
being watchful in
it with thanksgiving.

Colossians 4:2

Day

24 | Prayer Starts with a Thankful Heart

Why do we pray? Is it to ask for more or to change the course of the future? The older I get, the more I have come to realize that prayer is far less of a request and more of a response to what God has already done. Prayer is an attitude of gratitude, an unveiling of our weakness, and an active plea for God to do His will. Prayer starts with the recognition that we are dependent beings, not the driving force behind the universe. We can truly find the beauty of prayer when our hearts are bent toward thankfulness, whether we receive the biggest promotion or experience the simple joy of waking up each day (what a gift to be alive!).

Our satisfaction is not in what we are able to accomplish or claim, but in the beautiful paradox that God allows us to know His goodness and experience His love. Many days, we forget how little we can accomplish apart from His grace. We take glory in our strengths and forget all our abilities come from Him in the first place. We push God aside and claim the throne of our hearts, attempting to rule what little of this kingdom we think we can control. But we were not made to rule; we were made to worship.

If we are honest, many of us neglect the discipline of prayer not because we don't have the words to say, but because of a lack of thankfulness. But the gift of grace is just that—a gift. Our response to such a gift should never be a shout of self-worth, a proclamation of piety, or a recognition of righteous standing. The good we see and know and enjoy is because of His grace—it is all from Him! From that fountain of grace should explode, in each one of us, a heart of gratitude and humility, joy and praise.

Our prayers should be an outpouring of thankfulness, a place to meet with the God who has already given so much. So don't grow callous to the gift He has given. Let your prayers flow from a joyfully dependent heart.

Pray | *God, reveal to me where I have grown dependent on my own ability. Convict me when I have placed too much glory on myself. Help me to be thankful for Your gift of grace and to respond in joyful worship.*

For the moment all discipline seems painful rather than pleasant, but later it yields the peaceful fruit of righteousness to those who have been trained by it.

Hebrews 12:11

Discipline > Distraction

Have you noticed how easy it is to escape awkward silences these days? We can quickly transform any moment of discomfort with the handy-dandy smartphone, always at the ready to calm our social unease. Just the same, we've replaced deep conversations with scrolling social media. We've replaced quiet reflection with podcasts and music in our ears. Boredom has all but become a foreign concept. In our desperate pursuit of entertainment, technology has become a crutch to escape reality. We use it to pull our minds away from the stress of everyday living; but in the process, we have removed ourselves from the fruitful discipline of spending time with God.

In our haste, many of our prayers have become shortened, our focus has become blurred, and our desire for growth has been all but forgotten. When we choose distraction over discipline, we set ourselves up to fall into the routine of mediocrity and slowly become comfortable with glossing over the importance of God's presence in our lives.

In Christ, we are not called to be mediocre, and we certainly are not called to an underwhelming experience of what He gives. The God of grace is giving Himself to us—fully, completely, and abundantly. Are distractions so important that we would miss out on the fulfillment of knowing Him?

Discipline is necessary and beneficial. Instead of starting your day with a mental checkout—checking for updates on the socials or the latest news, find ways to practically walk in worship. Wake up and sing your favorite hymn. Set aside a time to engage in God's Word. Ask a friend how they are doing and really listen to the answer. Drive with the radio off and use that time to pray.

Don't let distraction rule your days. There is far too much joy to experience in the discipline of His grace.

What are practical disciplines you could add to your routine to focus more on God? How can you set barriers on screen time to help you center on spiritual discipline?

Many are the plans
in the mind
of a man, but
it is the purpose
of the Lord
that will stand.
Proverbs 19:21

He Is the Hero

How about a throwback question: If you could have any superpower, which one would you pick? I always go with the ability to fly (not to save the world or anything; it would just be nice to avoid rush-hour traffic!).

Superpowers (and jokes) aside, to some degree, we all hope to be our own sort of hero. We want to be the one everyone knows, the one who lives a life of great and lasting impact, and the one whose name will be remembered. Deep down, most of us have the dream that we will be the ones to make a difference.

But somewhere along the way, we have forgotten that we weren't called to be the hero—Jesus has already filled that role. He stepped into our mess not only to mend our broken hearts, but to gracefully make us new. Our response, then, should not be to be known, but to be faithful.

We are called to walk in the everyday ordinary and to reflect His grace along the way. We should not be overly concerned with impact or influence, but with simply loving the people God has given us to love. If your prayer is *God, I want to be used for great things*, try starting with something smaller. Instead of obsessing over opportunities that are big and flashy, look down your street, to the homes beside you, and to the lives that are already divinely intertwined with yours.

Many of us equate greatness with those who have the biggest impact or who have amassed the greatest following. Why value faithfulness when showmanship rules the world? But never underestimate the power of a faithful life. Don't underestimate the difference you make when you lace up your shoes every morning and choose to follow Jesus. Don't take for granted what God can do in the quiet of your ordinary day.

Strive for faithfulness. Find joy in the beauty of everyday things. Let Jesus be the hero. And be blown away when He does something through you that you never could have imagined on your own.

Reflect | *What is a practical way you can let go of the pride of recognition? What are a few ways you could serve someone or show love to a friend without anyone else knowing? Try this: Look for acts of kindness that aren't glamorous or social-media worthy.*

Rejoice in the Lord always; again I will say, rejoice.

Philippians 4:4

He Gives Joy for Today

One morning, I was taking the kids to school (late again, of course) when we hit completely stopped traffic barely a mile from our house. Up ahead, an eighteen-wheel-truck driver was trying to back into a narrow driveway off a two-lane road with no shoulder.

I started to let my running-late-again stress get the best of me, a mouthful of complaints waiting to jump across my lips. But instead, I took a breath, unlocked my vise grip on the steering wheel, and prayed. With a clear mind, I was able to use the moment of inconvenience as a teaching moment. I talked with the kids about the complexity of the driver's job and how much skill it would take to complete the seemingly impossible task. Frustration turned to fandom as we all started cheering for the driver to accomplish his goal. And on about the ninth try, he got that big ol' trailer exactly where it needed to go.

We all have moments that don't go according to plan. Sometimes it's a roadblock, and other times it's sick kids or jury duty. But through it all, God gives us enough grace to see the bigger picture. Stepping back from the stress of the moment reminds us that we can see the world through grace-colored glasses. From that perspective, it is much easier to remember the comforting truth that God is with us each moment of the day. In His nearness, He pours out His grace—and we have to choose whether our actions will reflect the same.

So rejoice in His grace, in the good moments and the bad. Live in the reminder that He is near, filling us with enough grace to share with those around us. There are enough hard things in this world, so let's be people who focus on His grace.

What gets under your skin throughout the day? How can you prepare yourself to respond in prayer instead of in frustration? How has the reality of God's joy changed your outlook on life?

And God is able to make all grace abound to you, so that having all sufficiency in all things at all times, you may abound in every good work.

2 Corinthians 9:8

Dip into His Grace

I heard a story once about a man who painted lines for the state transportation department (this was way back when lines were painted by hand—that is, if this story is even true). His first day on the job, he painted two miles of road lines—a record for the local road crew. Surprisingly, the second day he only made it a mile; and on the third, less than half a mile. After work on the third day, his boss asked him what had happened to his record-setting pace. The man looked at his boss and said, "Well, every day I get further and further from my paint bucket."

A bad story (or a great dad joke), yes. But it does convey an important point. Often, we approach our spiritual goals like the road painter, dipping into God's grace only to step as far as we possibly can before we must run back to refill. We paint until our brush bristles are wiry and frayed, only to look back and see that we've left God far behind. But here is the simple truth we often forget: That bucket of grace is easy to carry as we go.

For those of us who are task-oriented, we experience a constant pressure to do enough. *If I love God, then I have to be busy!* But remember the dipping is just as important as the painting. We can't serve well when our brush is dry. When you feel the burden to work your way into God's favor, remember that His love is not measured by the tasks we are able to get done. Sure, God has called us to do good works, but He never asked us to do them in our own strength. He invites us to work alongside Him, in the provision of His joy, by the power of His strength. He is our sustenance, never short on supply—we just have to make sure to fill up in His grace. So carry your brush, but don't forget your bucket.

Pray

Lord, help me trust in Your ability and not my own. Remind me of the grace that You abundantly supply. Give me the strength to step forward in kindness toward others and to reflect Your joy.

PART 3

Showing God's Grace

Be kind to one another, tenderhearted, forgiving one another, as God in Christ forgave you.

Ephesians 4:32

29 | Reflect His Joy

Negativity can be hard to escape sometimes. Between gloomy news headlines and pessimism all over social media, you don't have to look far to find something discouraging. And perhaps that's because we are far more prone to react to the bad than to search for the positive. But just because something is the quick and easy option doesn't make it the best.

When you think about it, most of the things we complain or worry about are beyond our ability to control or change. After all, we can't solve the world's problems, shorten the wait at the drive-thru, or make that person we hurt forgive us. What we *can* do is adopt a posture of joy even amid all the hard stuff. We can choose to walk in the hope that comes through Christ and move forward against any opposition with an attitude of thankfulness. Instead of complaining (even if it feels justified!), we can proclaim the blessings Christ has granted us. We can choose to proclaim hope to those around us with a smile and a listening ear. We can choose to proclaim and see the good instead of letting the bad consume us with worry.

Hard knocks will always be a part of reality. We can't escape the bad, but we don't have to be consumed by it. Instead of gossiping about a friend, find someone to encourage. Rather than railing at the news, go for a walk outside and talk to a stranger. When that coworker gets on your nerves, pray for patience and spend time with them anyway. Through the grace of God, we can use our words, attitudes, and actions to reflect Christ's joy day after day.

Reflect | *Are you a complainer or a proclaimer? How can you complain less and proclaim His grace more? List three things that you tend to complain about and then list three ways you can find the good in those moments.*

Whoever finds his life will lose it, and whoever loses his life for my sake will find it.

Matthew 10:39

30 | Lose Yourself

Have you ever looked back at an old picture of yourself and thought, *Who is that!?*

From season to season, the way our personalities change can be quite something to behold. For much of my life, I was quiet and reserved, but now I'll jump into just about any conversation. Fast food used to be my bread and butter (get it?), but these days it's healthy eating all the way. Essentially, all of our choices and habits and mannerisms are a reflection of who we are, a curation of our own personal pizzazz. But does following Jesus mean we have to give all our uniqueness away? Do we have to fit a certain mold or denomination or class to fit into the narrative of His story? How can we still *be* ourselves and *lose* ourselves at the same time?

Listen, following Jesus does not mean you can't keep your quirks (it's okay to be weird). When we give up our lives, we aren't surrendering our uniqueness; we are surrendering our stubbornness. Jesus isn't asking you to give up your personality, just your pride.

God created you to be you, but He also created you to see the bigger picture. God did not form us to spend our whole lives discovering ourselves only to feel like something is missing. Really, God has made us—and invited us—to discover Him.

In our giving ourselves up, He is constantly refining and replacing our callousness with care and our selfishness with a desire to serve. Jesus doesn't take away our style, but He does change our hearts. He allows us to be unique all while shaping us into His likeness, sanctifying us as we grow in grace. You can enjoy being you, while still remembering exactly who He made you to be.

When we lose ourselves, we find our greatest sense of worth is not limited to who we are today. Our true and lasting value comes from seeing and experiencing and knowing His grace. Lose yourself in His grace and you will be amazed at what you find.

Pray | *God, help me to be fully myself in Your grace. Give me a vision of Your kingdom over my own. Help me to lose myself, that I might show more of Your grace.*

Mercy triumphs over judgment.

James 2:13

31 | Judging Others Empties You

Our backyard is full of trees. When we first moved in, it looked like a jungle, with vines and brambles thick as cold molasses. I was determined to clear the mess, and slowly, section by section, I worked my way through the tangled weeds to tame what had become drastically overgrown. But here's the thing about weeds: If you fail to keep them under control, they will grow right back.

You may not have a backyard forest to manage, but we all have hearts that are excellent at metaphorical overgrowth. As it is, judging others is one of those spiritual weeds that remains the hardest to keep cut down. It may begin as just a sprout, but if we give it room to run, it will soon take over every inch of our hearts.

At the start, judging others can feel good or even validating (we all think we're great, right?). But ultimately, our judgments rob us of joy and suck us dry with envy and disdain. Though it is in our nature to self-elevate, God calls us to a better way. Instead of growing the weeds of judgment, He calls us to grow fruitful gardens of mercy, showing others the same grace He has shown us.

Practically, there is no shame in asking God for some weed management—to clear out your heart where the habit of judging has overgrown. We must keep in mind that everyone has an embarrassing story, a shameful past, or a current struggle. We all have flaws that can be easily pointed out, but God does not encourage us to make others feel small or unworthy. He calls us to love, to show mercy to those who have failed, and to give grace to those who are struggling.

So cut back your judgments and keep growing in grace.

Reflect | *How have you seen or experienced God's mercy in your own life? How can you reciprocate His mercy to others? Is there anyone you need to apologize to for judging too harshly?*

If we live by
the Spirit,
Let us also keep
in step with
the Spirit.
Galatians 5:25

Experience Through Obedience

If you read one hundred books on the Grand Canyon, you might be filled with knowledge, but until you visit, you would never feel the awesome wonder of staring into the unfathomable abyss of an endless red and brown chasm stretching as far as the eye can see. You would never feel your pounding heart as you stepped to look over the edge. Words simply cannot replace the experience. The Grand Canyon exudes a certain majesty, and no matter how good a description you might hear or read, you have to see it to really experience it.

The point is this: Everything beneficial involves application. If we want to feel God's grace in our lives, we have to understand His truth. We have to search the wonderful depth of His Word, we have to stand on the ledge of faith, and we have to listen for His response in steadfast prayer.

Just as a visit to the Grand Canyon is crucial to understanding its grandeur, so obedience is the key to our experience of God. If we claim to live by the Spirit but continually disobey, and if we claim to walk with the Spirit but waver in our steps, then we will miss the blessings of following Jesus.

We don't have to wonder who God is or resign ourselves to guess what knowing Him is like. He *wants* us to experience His grace! He is deeply personal, but to experience Him personally, we have to be willing to commit to Him our choices, our aspirations, and our dreams. We don't need to settle for head knowledge of God when He offers to captivate our hearts.

Sure, you can know about God, but what would your life look like if your pursuit of Him became less about learning and more about living? How would your choices be different when guided by His Spirit or when walking in obedience—not as a way to follow the rules, but as a way to see more of His love? He is giving us His grace, full stop, with no interruptions or exclusions. Press into daily obedience and see for yourself the wonder of following Jesus.

Meditate | *Read Galatians 5. How can you practically apply Spirit-led obedience in your life? What fruit do you hope to see as you obey?*

Little children, let us not love in word or talk but in deed and in truth.

1 John 3:18

Small Moments, Big Difference

Lately I've been working on my jump shot. Now let me be clear, I have never been a good basketball player. But our boys wanted to learn the game, so on most days, you can find us in the driveway, hour after hour, working on skills (you should see my hook shot now!). These driveway practices may seem like small, unimportant moments. After all, it's just basketball, right? But small moments matter.

Our character is most defined in moments of trivial simplicity—in deed and in truth. We can learn about God all day, but until we apply what we know in the unattractive ordinary, we are missing the point. God's grace has a changing factor and it should reach into every aspect of who we are. Knowing Him is not limited to facts and precepts; knowing Him is centered on becoming *like* Him.

With that in mind, we can look at each small moment as an opportunity to reflect His grace. Maybe it's in the driveway catching rebounds or at the table sharing bread. Maybe it's in your social media interaction or your tone in conversations. Wherever you are, your actions in the minuscule moments are where others see God's grace in you the most.

Have you ever stopped to think that your friends can see Jesus through the way you live? Discipleship 101, my friend. Carving out time to love those around you, meeting needs, teaching values, caring about things that might not seem to matter on the surface, and living each moment in His grace. This is where we make an impact. In the quiet of the relationships we pour into, when we give ourselves in love.

Big moments are sure to come, but don't sit around waiting. There is so much joy in the teaching and learning and loving that come from those small, quiet, ordinary days. So live out His grace in all you do.

Reflect

How can you see your small moments in a big way? What normal activities can you use to point others to the grace of Jesus?

Jesus said to him, "I do not say to you seven times, but seventy-seven times."

Matthew 18:22

Day

34

Forgiveness Is Not Yours to Withhold

"Lord, how many times must I forgive?"

Jesus answered the question, "I do not say to you seven times, but seventy-seven times." His response was not to keep a tally of how many times you should forgive until you reach the limit. Quite the opposite. His answer shows that forgiveness should be given freely, not withheld or rationed. His response is a spotlight on the elephant in the room—we all have been forgiven beyond what we could ever deserve. In response to the grace that has been poured out on our lives, in response to the mercy God has shown, in response to the compassion He constantly gives, how could we possibly *not* forgive those who do us wrong?

But what happens when we catch that one friend in a lie? What happens when that friend leaves us out of the next hangout or replies with a hurtful response? At some point, we all ask the question: *There has to be a limit on forgiveness, right?*

News flash: People are going to let you down. But if you are going to succeed in grace-filled relationships, you can't turn your back when things get hard or uncomfortable. Neither can you afford revenge in your repertoire. Live in grace, not in a grudge!

If we are going to show His grace, we have to continually forgive. We don't need to keep count or try to balance the scales—we can forgive freely, just as God has forgiven us. Forgiveness may not be easy, but there is a freedom that follows our willingness to surrender. So learn to give second chances, time and time again.

Meditate | *Read Matthew 18:21–35. What makes practical forgiveness so hard? Why is it so important that we continually forgive?*

Above all these
put on love,
which binds
everything together
in perfect harmony.

Colossians 3:14

Day

35 | Love Is Wearable

I've been trying to figure out how to stop our dog from digging holes in the yard. He's turned into an excavator extraordinaire. I saw a video that black pepper works as a deterrent, but I don't know if I could grind a half acre's worth. At that point, the birds would sneeze any time they flew over our yard!

Here's the point I'm digging at: We are always looking for a quick fix to bad habits, but this predicament goes far beyond our wayward pets. The same goes for me and you. We often approach our bad habits from the standpoint of crisis avoidance instead of crisis resolution. It would take too much work to actually change the behavior, so we resolve to distract ourselves and just hope we won't fall back into our old ways. The hard part is, we live in a yard of opportunity, and there's always a place to dig another hole.

So what's the fix? How do we recenter our lives around real change and not just Band-Aid repair? How do we change our habits to reflect God's grace in our choices?

We put on love.

I know, that sounds too easy, too simple, and too elementary. Paradoxically, the whole point of the upside-down gospel is this truth: We love ourselves best when we love others first. If we want to see change, we have to walk in a reality where we are not so consumed with the idolized "me." Instead of "God, give me," we should be saying, "God, how can I give myself away?" Instead of letting self-serving habits rule our routine, we should submit to service and love. When we seek His Spirit, His promise is not to patch our broken seams, but to make us completely new.

The fix for our lives is found in following God's way. Changing our routine or daily activities will only get us so far. If we want real change, we have to encounter real grace.

So put on love like a pair of pants in the morning. Make love a habit that you can't live without. Look people in the eye and encourage them often. Step out from behind your screen and give someone a hug. Take on each day with the joy and freedom that Jesus brings.

How can you wear God's love today? How can you be more consistent in seeking grace-filled change? How free do you feel to love others without expectations?

Therefore encourage one another and build one another up, just as you are doing.

1 Thessalonians 5:11

Day

36 | Build Each Other Up

"You do good work."

Everyone has those core memories that make a lasting impact. My grandfather's words have always stuck with me and will continue to stand out for the rest of my life. For me, spending a Saturday morning with my dad and grandpa to work on lawnmowers led to the encouraging words that continually motivate me to do my best. I doubt either of them remembers all those moments, but I always will.

Encouragement is a huge factor in our response to God's grace. When we live in response to what we have received, our common interaction with others should be to encourage and exhort. We have the opportunity in every conversation to show the love of Jesus. We have the chance in all our relationships to convey the grace God has given.

Giving encouragement may take a little extra effort and attention, but the impact certainly goes a long way. With just a little focus, a few kind words can make the difference in a person's day. All it takes is a little phrase like "Keep up the good work!" or "Those shoes are awesome!" or "Thanks for being my friend." Truthfully, we never know the impact our encouragement will bring. A few kind words could last a lifetime.

So let's be hope and light, vessels of grace in a sea of despair. Let's shine with joy and reflect compassion and kindness. Let's build each other up. Our words are weighty, but they don't have to be heavy or harsh. May we constantly share the grace we have in Jesus through our encouraging words.

 Reflect | *Who can you encourage today? How can you incorporate encouragement into your regular routine? Call a friend today and lift them up!*

Welcome one another
as Christ has
welcomed you,
for the glory of God.

Romans 15:7

Day 37 | Hospitality Begins in the Heart

My brother and I were driving home one night and saw a car stranded on the road—a classic VW Beetle. Upon pulling over to help, we realized the gentleman had a flat tire, but no jack to lift his car. I looked at my brother and said, "I think we can pick this thing up." We reached down, grabbed the bumper, and with an extraordinary heave, lifted the man's car.

Now I'm not suggesting you try this at home, but I do want you to hear this: You do not need the most to be a good host! The tools of hospitality are not found in the niceness of your home or the neatness of your life, but in the readiness of your hands. Often our hopes of hospitality become dashed when we feel like our lives are a bit too messy and our schedules are totally too busy. Finding a place for hospitality can be a real hurdle, but it can also be an incredible blessing.

Our perspective on hospitality shifts when we highlight it with God's grace. Hospitality is not only defined by inviting people over for fancy special occasions. Hospitality is a mindset that marks our perspective and a constant awareness of how we can demonstrate practical love toward strangers and friends.

The way we interact with others should be a reflection of the way God has welcomed us, even when we were the least deserving. He not only welcomes us, but He also adopts us as sons and daughters, welcoming us into His family as His own. How, then, do we show a similar grace toward others? Is it possible to be welcoming and hospitable—even if it feels uncomfortable or strange?

To be people known as hospitable is a dream worth pursuing. Defined not by stereotypes or cultural standards, but by saving grace. We can be the ones who talk less about politics and more about how we can help each other. We can be the ones who focus less on differences and more on how needs can be met. We can be a people who love genuinely, just as God has so graciously loved us.

Meditate

Read Romans 15:1–7. How does this passage encourage you to engage with others? How can hospitality be applied to your everyday life?

Do justice...
love kindness...
walk humbly
with your God.

Micah 6:8

38 | God Can Change the World

Have you ever sat in a math class and wondered, *When am I ever going to use this?* (Good news—I used the Pythagorean theorem in real life once!) Truthfully, we can experience an overwhelming sense of frustration when we fail to see how our learning is applied. So let's skip the philosophical and jump straight to the practical—God is at work in the world and He is faithful to redeem.

Don't believe me? Look around! He is in each sunrise, in the high fives of friends, and in all the love we show others. Our faith is not a metaphorical mystery. God does not leave us alone to try and figure everything out. Our response to His grace plays out in this obvious way: What we believe should affect how we live out each day of our lives. So let's be practical!

If we are going to apply God's love, we must choose kindness over callousness. We must pursue justice over judgment, mercy over malice. We can engage with others in light of what God has done for us and show His love in tangible ways. Daily we can wake up renewed so we can give ourselves away—not as a means of defeat, but as a means of surrender. We lay down our arms and admit that, in our own strength, we don't have the means to fix this world. We hold tightly to His grace, understanding that by His power, He *can* fix the world.

The burden to fix it all is not on us, but we can rejoice in the knowledge that God invites us to partner in what He is doing. So we trust that He is in control and we can take each day as it comes. We have the opportunity every hour to witness His faithfulness and to share His blessings. So let's roll up our sleeves and join in His work.

Pray | *God, help me see the needs around me. Encourage me to serve those I can help. Help me to see the work You are faithfully doing and show me how to join in.*

He who calls you is faithful; he will surely do it.

1 Thessalonians 5:24

Day 39 | Sanctification Is a Journey

Most of us are probably familiar with the feeling of hitting the gym as a New Year's resolution, or deciding to conquer all our bad eating habits in grandiose fashion. But after the hype wears off and the soreness takes hold, a subtle thought starts to creep in: "What's the point of suffering if I am not going to see results?"

To find results, we first have to come to terms with humility, recognizing that change happens over time, on the building blocks of consistency. Every day is not a motivator. Every push to be better does not come with the satisfaction of progress. But there is always purpose in the process.

Just the same, we can't rush what God is doing in our lives. Sanctification is a journey, a molding and refining. It may be slow in coming, but we shouldn't doubt the progress God is making in us. We walk by the Spirit, patiently pursuing righteousness, daily coming back with the realization that we will need His grace all over again.

If you have gotten into a health kick or an exercise routine, you know the struggle to keep on track. There is always an excuse to not go to the gym or eat the right thing. Often it feels like conditions have to be perfect before the choice can even be made (I mean, no way I'm running outside if it's raining or cold). But you don't have to have perfect conditions to pursue God's grace. He already knows our imperfections. So relax in His presence and treasure the time you are committing to Him. All you need to do is give Him yourself, and He will take care of the rest.

We surrender in our inability today, and gladly we can surrender again tomorrow. Take hold of the glorious truth that God does not measure us by our mistakes, He measures us by His unending grace. So be consistent in your approach. Enjoy the journey and trust Him with the results.

What progress have you seen God making in your life? How has He changed your heart over the last few weeks, months, or even years? What do you hope God will do in the future?

Let your manner of life be worthy of the gospel of Christ.

Philippians 1:27

Day 40 | He Has Called You

Once every few years I make a point to reread *The Lord of the Rings*. Even though I've read the series many times, somehow these books remain just as captivating as ever. One of my favorite elements in the story is the pull the characters continually feel to be somewhere else. The innkeepers, or those who stay behind, long to see the world, while the hobbits (with hungry bellies) longingly wish to be home. The first longs for a bit of adventure in the unknown, while the other longs for a soft bed and a warm fire. Though perhaps envious of the other at times, they remain dependent on each other, with neither able to fulfill their calling without the other. For what good is an inn without a traveler? And how would one travel if along the road there were no place to stay? They need each other, even if they sometimes want to *be* each other.

We may not have real "innkeepers" anymore, but where do you find yourself in the story? Whether you consider yourself an innkeeper or a traveler or something in between, as we close out this journey through God's grace, the final takeaway is that there is immense value in who God has made you to be. We may want to be like another person, or on some days we may be jealous of what God has given to our friends (or even foes). But the value of our purpose is not based on what we have, how popular we are, or what level of success we achieve. Rather, our value is defined by how God sees us, how He has called us, and how we can love, serve, and lead those around us.

No matter your dwelling or occupation, your fame or fortune, you have a purpose and potential in response to what God has done and is doing through you. Yes, He has called *you*! You have been made to deeply love. Your purpose is not rooted in external variables, but in your inward recognition of God's perfect promise. Your fulfillment is not based on where you have been called, but on how you can find His joy in it.

Reflect | *Remember God's love with gladness when you forgive, when you set time aside to pray, and when you show hospitality to others. Speak His love with the words you say and show His love in the small ways you obey. Each day is a new day to slow down and experience all He has to offer. Live out your calling in His abundant grace.*

Abundant Grace

All Scripture quotations are taken from the ESV® Bible (The Holy Bible, English Standard Version®), copyright © 2001 by Crossway, a publishing ministry of Good News Publishers. Used by permission. All rights reserved.

Hardcover ISBN 978-0-593-58141-4

Copyright © 2024 by Will and Courtney Kassner

Text by Will Kassner
Illustrations and calligraphy by Courtney Kassner
Cover and interior design by Danielle Deschenes

Published in the United States by WaterBrook, an imprint of Random House, a division of Penguin Random House LLC.

Ink & Willow® and its colophon are registered trademarks of Penguin Random House LLC.

Printed in China

2024—First Edition

WaterBrookMultnomah.com

10 9 8 7 6 5 4 3 2 1

SPECIAL SALES Most WaterBrook and Ink & Willow books are available at special quantity discounts when purchased in bulk by corporations, organizations, and special-interest groups. Custom imprinting or excerpting can also be done to fit special needs. For information, please email specialmarketscms@penguinrandomhouse.com.